"Homeless to Hollywood" is not just a story; it's an inspiring journey of resilience, dreams realized, and the transformative power of art. This book invites you to witness Richard Hutchins' odyssey, a testament to the indomitable human spirit that refuses to give up, no matter the challenges. Purchase your copy and embark on a voyage of hope, redemption, and the extraordinary power of the human spirit.

"Homeless to Hollywood: The Artful Triumph of Richard Hutchins" - Book Outline

I. Introduction

Brief overview of Richard Hutchins' journey
Setting the stage for the transformation from homelessness to artistic success

II. Chapter 1: Skid Row Nights

Exploring Richard's early struggles on Skid Row
Describing the challenges of living on the streets
Introducing the concept of art as an escape

III. Chapter 2: Encounter with Destiny

Narrating the fateful meeting with Charlie Rocket and the Dreamr team
Detailing the Dream Machine Tour and its impact on Richard's life

IV. Chapter 3: Dreams on Canvas

Discussing Richard's artistic process and techniques
Highlighting his unique use of unconventional materials like M&M's and Skittles

Introduction

Once upon a time, in the bustling streets of Skid Row, where hope seemed like a distant memory, a remarkable story began to unfold—the story of Richard Hutchins. It's a tale that defies the odds, where the extraordinary triumphs over the ordinary, and the canvas of life transforms from shades of despair to vibrant hues of success.

Richard's journey commenced on the unforgiving streets of Skid Row, where survival often took precedence over dreams. These alleys, witness to countless struggles, would soon become the backdrop for a story of resilience, passion, and unwavering determination.

As we embark on this narrative, picture the dimly lit corners of Skid Row—the makeshift shelters, the struggles for survival, and the echoes of dreams that refuse to fade away. Richard's early days were filled with challenges that seemed insurmountable, yet within the confines of adversity, seeds of an artistic revolution were quietly taking root.

But this is not just a story of hardships; it's a testament to the human spirit's ability to rise above circumstances. The stage is set not just in the shadows of Skid Row but also in the gleaming lights of Hollywood, where dreams are not only realized but celebrated.

Imagine the contrast as we transition from the gritty streets to the glamorous world of art galleries in Beverly Hills—a journey that mirrors the transformation of Richard's life. In these luxurious settings, his artwork, once a means of escape, now adorns the walls alongside those of renowned artists, capturing the attention of celebrities and influencers from around the world.

The Introduction invites you to step into Richard's world—a world where homelessness is not the end but a challenging chapter in a remarkable odyssey. As we turn the pages, anticipate the unveiling of a story that transcends the conventional, a story that resonates with anyone who has faced adversity and dared to dream.

Get ready to witness the extraordinary journey of a man who turned the darkest shades of his life into vibrant strokes of success. "Homeless to Hollywood" is not just a story; it's an invitation to explore the limitless possibilities that emerge when the human spirit refuses to be confined by circumstances. So, fasten your seatbelts, and let's embark on a journey of hope, transformation, and the artful triumph of Richard Hutchins.

Chapter 1: Skid Row Nights

In the heart of Los Angeles, where the glittering lights of Hollywood seem like a distant mirage, there lies a place called Skid Row—an unforgiving realm where dreams fade away amidst the struggles for survival. This is where our journey with Richard Hutchins truly begins.

Early Struggles: A Canvas of Challenges

Picture the bustling streets of Skid Row, where Richard's journey took its initial steps. These streets were not merely pathways; they were the testing grounds of resilience. Richard faced challenges that were both harsh and unrelenting. The nights were long, and the days seemed even longer as he navigated the concrete jungle, searching for a glimmer of hope.

Living on the Streets: The Harsh Realities

Skid Row, with its makeshift shelters and the constant hustle for survival, is a place that tests the mettle of those who tread its alleys. The challenges of living on the streets are multifaceted—finding shelter, securing a meal, and safeguarding personal belongings become daily battles. Skid Row's harsh embrace leaves an indelible mark on those who call it home.

Art as an Escape: Painting a New Reality

In the midst of the concrete and chaos, Richard discovered an escape—a sanctuary not built with bricks but with strokes of a paintbrush. Art became more than a form of expression; it became a lifeline. s.

The very streets that echoed with hardship were transformed into a canvas of possibilities. Richard's art was not just a creation; it was a manifestation of resilience, a testament to the human spirit's ability to find beauty in the bleakest of circumstances

In this chapter, we delve into the raw and poignant details of Richard's early days on Skid Row. It's a story of survival, painted against a backdrop of adversity, where the concept of art as an escape emerged as a guiding light. As we turn the pages, be prepared to witness the transformation of struggle into artistry, despair into hope, and Skid Row nights into the first strokes of a masterpiece. The journey has just begun, and the canvas is vast with potential.

Chapter 2: Encounter with Destiny

In the grand tapestry of life, some moments stand out like vivid brushstrokes, altering the course of one's journey. For Richard Hutchins, such a moment unfolded in a serendipitous encounter that would change the trajectory of his life forever.

Narrating the Fateful Meeting: A Twist of Fate

Picture a typical day in Los Angeles—a city that thrives on hustle and dreams. It was on such a day that Richard's path intersected with destiny. Enter Charlie Rocket and the Dreamr team, catalysts of change on a mission to breathe life into dreams.

The meeting was not just a casual exchange; it was a cosmic alignment, a convergence of stories waiting to be written. As Richard navigated the streets, little did he know that the blue truck that pulled up would usher in a tidal wave of transformation.

The Dream Machine Tour: A Journey Beyond Boundaries

The Dream Machine Tour was not just a tour; it was an odyssey of hope, a caravan of dreams crisscrossing the country. Detailing this extraordinary journey, we witness Richard becoming an integral part of a movement that transcended geographical boundaries.

Charlie Rocket and his team, armed with a vision to make dreams tangible, embarked on a 100,000-mile journey. Through cities and towns, the Dreamr team unleashed the magic of hope, and in the heart of Los Angeles, they found Richard—a man with dreams as vast as the California sky.

Impact on Richard's Life: A Second Chance to Dream

The Dream Machine Tour wasn't just about miles covered; it was about the miles traveled within the hearts of those it touched. Richard's life, once confined to the struggles of Skid Row, underwent a metamorphosis. It was more than just art supplies and a hundred-dollar bill; it was a second chance to pursue the dreams that had simmered within him.

In this chapter, we unravel the threads of fate that brought Richard face-to-face with Charlie Rocket and the Dreamr team. It's a narrative of cosmic alignment, where a chance encounter becomes the genesis of a life-altering journey. The Dream Machine Tour was not just a tour—it was a conduit for dreams, and Richard's encounter with destiny was the prelude to a symphony of transformation. The canvas is now set for the strokes of change, and Richard is ready to paint his dreams into reality.

Chapter 3: Dreams on Canvas

Artistry, like life, is a canvas waiting to be adorned with colors and tales. In this chapter, we delve into the enchanting world of Richard Hutchins' creative genius—a world where dreams come alive on canvas.

Artistic Process: The Symphony of Creation

Imagine stepping into Richard's studio, a space pulsating with creativity. His artistic process is a symphony—a carefully orchestrated dance of inspiration, passion, and raw emotion. It begins with a blank canvas, a realm of possibilities awaiting his touch.

Richard's approach to art is not confined by rules; it's an expression that transcends boundaries. From the first stroke to the final flourish, each movement is a testament to his connection with the canvas. We explore the rhythm of his artistic process—a dance that transforms imagination into tangible beauty.

Unconventional Materials: A Palette of Surprises

What sets Richard apart is not just his artistic flair but his willingness to embrace the unexpected. Enter the unconventional materials—M&M's, Skittles, and a dash of audacity. Richard's palette extends beyond traditional paints, turning everyday items into instruments of artistic expression.

Skittles become bursts of vibrant color, and M&M's transform into textured landscapes. The use of unconventional materials is not merely a choice; it's a statement—a rebellion against artistic norms, a celebration of creativity unbridled.

Crafting Dreams with Color and Texture

Richard's art is not just about what meets the eye; it's a sensory experience. Close your eyes and imagine the tactile journey—textures that invite touch, colors that evoke emotion. The canvas becomes a dreamscape, a portal into Richard's visions and aspirations.

In this chapter, we navigate the labyrinth of Richard's artistic mind, exploring the intricacies of his creative process. It's a journey of color and texture, of breaking free from artistic conventions, and of dreams taking shape on a canvas that knows no bounds. The palette is eclectic, the strokes are bold, and the result is a collection of masterpieces that transcend the limits of imagination. As we journey through the realm of Dreams on Canvas, be prepared to witness art not just as a visual spectacle but as an immersive experience—one that reflects the dreams that inspired its creation.

In this chapter, we navigate the labyrinth of Richard's artistic mind, exploring the intricacies of his creative process. It's a journey of color and texture, of breaking free from artistic conventions, and of dreams taking shape on a canvas that knows no bounds. The palette is eclectic, the strokes are bold, and the result is a collection of masterpieces that transcend the limits of imagination. As we journey through the realm of Dreams on Canvas, be prepared to witness art not just as a visual spectacle but as an immersive experience—one that reflects the dreams that inspired its creation.

Chapter 4: The Art Show that Changed Everything

In the glitzy enclave of Beverly Hills, where dreams often materialize in shades of opulence, Richard Hutchins' art took center stage in a show that would redefine his destiny. This chapter unfolds the captivating tale of the LOVE & DREAMS art show—an event that etched its mark on the canvas of Richard's life.

Recalling the Spectacle: LOVE & DREAMS in Beverly Hills

Picture the Cool HeART Gallery, bathed in the warm glow of anticipation. It was at this venue that Richard's art stepped into the limelight, alongside two other prominent artists—Ruben Rojas and Richard Orlinski. The air was charged with excitement as the party began, accompanied by the rhythm of Montel Jordan's "This Is How I Do It."

As the doors opened, the room transformed into a haven of artistic celebration. Richard, now at the epicenter of attention, greeted eager fans, posed for countless photos, and reveled in the genuine warmth that permeated the atmosphere.

Celebrities and the Artistic Embrace

The LOVE & DREAMS art show was not just an exhibition; it was a spectacle that attracted the gaze of the stars. Will Smith, 2 Chainz, Steve Harvey—names that resonate with Hollywood glamour—all found themselves drawn to Richard's creations. His art became more than just visuals; it became a conversation piece, a narrative that transcended the boundaries of the canvas.

Oprah Winfrey, the epitome of influence and discernment, surprised Richard during an Entertainment Tonight interview. In a moment of pure admiration, she not only acknowledged his talent but became a collector, purchasing one of his pieces. The overwhelming response from celebrities wasn't just a nod to artistic brilliance; it was a testament to the transformative power of Richard's journey.

LOVE & DREAMS: A Red-Carpet Affair for Richard

The art show, aptly titled "LOVE & DREAMS: One Night to Change A Life," was more than just an exhibition; it was Richard's red-carpet affair. Each sale that night contributed to the narrative of change, echoing through the corridors of possibility. It was a night when the energy in the room pulsated with love—an organic symphony of genuine appreciation and support.

As we navigate through the recollections of this remarkable art show, be prepared to witness a turning point in Richard's journey. The canvas of his life expanded, adorned with the hues of recognition and celebrity endorsement. The LOVE & DREAMS art show wasn't just an event; it was a catalyst that propelled Richard from the periphery of Skid Row to the dazzling heights of Beverly Hills. The next chapter awaits, promising to unfold a narrative that transcends artistic boundaries and invites the world to witness the extraordinary evolution of Richard Hutchins.

Chapter 5: Oprah's Surprise

In the grand tapestry of unexpected moments, some shine brighter than the rest—moments that become chapters in the book of life. One such chapter unfolds in the wake of the LOVE & DREAMS art show, as we witness the awe-inspiring surprise that left both Richard Hutchins and the world at large speechless: Oprah's unexpected embrace of his art.

The Unexpected Encounter: A Meeting with Royalty

Imagine the scene—a buzzing Entertainment Tonight interview, cameras capturing the essence of Richard's journey. Little did he know that the interviewer had a surprise in store—a surprise that would elevate his story to the pinnacle of global recognition.

As the interview unfolded, a moment of pure magic materialized: Oprah Winfrey emerged, not just as a spectator but as a genuine admirer.

Oprah's surprise was not just a passing acknowledgment; it was a royal seal of approval. In that moment, a connection transcended the realms of celebrity and artist, as Oprah expressed not just admiration but a desire to own a piece of Richard's soulful creations. The unexpected purchase of his art became a testament to the universal language that art speaks—one that resonates with the hearts of individuals, regardless of their stature.

Reflecting on Global Recognition: The Oprah Effect

Oprah Winfrey, a name synonymous with influence and cultural impact, had not just entered Richard's world; she had become a patron of his art. The global recognition that followed was nothing short of extraordinary. Richard's creations, once confined to the walls of Skid Row, were now making waves on a global stage.

The impact of Oprah's surprise wasn't just felt in the echo chambers of Hollywood; it reverberated across continents. Richard's story became an inspiration, a beacon of hope for dreamers worldwide. The narrative shifted from Skid Row struggles to an artist whose work was endorsed by one of the most influential figures on the planet.

The Ripple Effect: Beyond Art and into Change

Oprah's surprise wasn't merely a transaction; it was a catalyst for change. The ripples of her endorsement reached far beyond the realms of art, touching the lives of those who resonated with Richard's journey. The narrative was no longer confined to the strokes of a paintbrush; it expanded into a universal story of resilience, transformation, and the boundless power of the human spirit.

In this chapter, we dive into the surprise that Oprah Winfrey brought into Richard Hutchins' life. It's a tale of recognition, not just for the art but for the indomitable spirit that forged it. As we explore the impact of Oprah's embrace, be prepared to witness the convergence of worlds—a moment that transcends celebrity culture and establishes Richard's art as a force capable of touching the very soul of humanity. The canvas of his life expands once more, inviting the world to witness the chapters yet to unfold.

Chapter 6: Life After the Spotlight

The glittering lights of Hollywood, the applause of celebrities, and the global recognition—all these elements that once illuminated Richard Hutchins' life became memories as the spotlight dimmed. Chapter 6 unfolds the narrative of life after the spectacle, exploring the emotional and practical dimensions of newfound success.

Adjusting to the New Normal: From Streets to Hollywood Hills

The transition from the bustling streets of Skid Row to the opulent expanse of Hollywood Hills marked a profound shift in Richard's life.

As the applause faded and the red carpets were rolled up, the reality of adjusting to this new normal set in. The streets were no longer his canvas; instead, the Hollywood Hills became the backdrop for a life transformed.

The process of finding a place to call home, navigating the intricacies of a transformed lifestyle, and grappling with the emotional shifts brought about by newfound success—all became part of the delicate dance of adjustment. Life after the spotlight was not just a continuation; it was a journey of acclimatization to a reality that seemed like a distant dream not so long ago.

Embracing Stability: Moving Beyond Skid Row

Life after the spotlight brought more than just physical relocation; it ushered in a sense of stability that Skid Row could never provide. Richard, once tethered to the uncertainties of homelessness, now found himself on the brink of a new chapter—a chapter that promised not just artistic success but a life of security and purpose.

The Hollywood Hills, adorned with luxury, became a testament to the resilience of a man who had weathered the storms of Skid Row. Adjusting to this newfound stability required not just a change in location but a recalibration of the mindset forged on the streets.

From Dreams to Reality: Owning a Home and a Future

The dreams that echoed through the corridors of Skid Row materialized in the form of keys to a new home. As Richard prepared to move into a place he could finally call his own, the emotional weight of this achievement was palpable. Life after the spotlight meant not just a change in circumstances; it was the embodiment of dreams that had been nurtured during the darkest nights.

In this chapter, we navigate through the emotional and practical intricacies of Richard Hutchins' life after the spotlight. It's a reflection on adjustment, stability, and the profound impact of realizing dreams.

As we witness the transformation from Skid Row to Hollywood Hills, the canvas of Richard's life expands once more, inviting us to explore the chapters that unfold when the applause fades and the artist is left with the silence of accomplishment.

Chapter 7: Giving Back

Amidst the acclaim and the newfound stability of Hollywood Hills, Richard Hutchins emerges not just as an artist but as a beacon of compassion. Chapter 7 delves into his commitment to giving back, showcasing initiatives that extend beyond the canvas to address homelessness and broader social issues.

A Commitment to Compassion: A Promise to Make a Difference

The journey from Skid Row to Hollywood Hills instilled in Richard a profound understanding of the struggles faced by those left behind on the streets. Armed with the transformative power of his own story, he embraced a commitment to compassion—a promise to make a difference in the lives of others.

Richard's giving back isn't a mere afterthought; it's a cornerstone of his newfound success. The Hollywood Hills may be a far cry from the streets of Skid Row, but the echoes of those struggles resonate in his commitment to uplifting those who still find themselves ensnared by the cycle of homelessness.

Initiatives to Address Homelessness: Beyond Art into Action

Giving back, for Richard, goes beyond the strokes of a paintbrush; it translates into tangible initiatives aimed at addressing the root causes of homelessness. From walking the sidewalks of Skid Row to advocating for change, Richard becomes a voice for those who often go unheard.

His initiatives range from providing immediate relief, such as distributing resources and funds, to actively participating in efforts to reshape policies and perceptions surrounding homelessness. The artist who once painted his dreams on envelopes now seeks to paint a brighter future for those in need.

A Vision for Change: Inspiring Others to Pay It Forward

The commitment to giving back is not a solitary endeavor for Richard; it's an invitation for others to join in the journey of change. By sharing his story, he sparks conversations about the transformative power of compassion and the impact one individual can have on an entire community.

In this chapter, we explore the multifaceted approach Richard takes in giving back. It's a narrative that extends beyond the canvas, intertwining with the very fabric of societal change. As we witness the artist turning philanthropist, the pages of Richard Hutchins' life story become a call to action—a reminder that success, when shared, has the power to shape not just individual destinies but the collective future of those touched by the artist's compassionate brush.

Chapter 8: The Pink Party and Future Aspirations

As the chapters of Richard Hutchins' extraordinary journey unfold, Chapter 8 invites us into the anticipation of upcoming events and offers a glimpse into the artist's aspirations for the future. The narrative shifts from the past and the present to the canvas of what lies ahead, painted with hues of hope, ambition, and a touch of the unexpected.

Previewing "The Pink Party": A Celebration of Purpose

Amidst the vibrant swirl of upcoming events, "The Pink Party" stands as a testament to Richard's commitment to meaningful causes. This chapter opens the door to the details of this remarkable event—an endeavor that goes beyond artistic celebration to benefit Breast Cancer Awareness month in October.

"The Pink Party" becomes not just an event on the calendar but a canvas on which Richard continues to paint purpose. With the support of The Dreamr Team, this initiative reflects his dedication to giving back, tying the threads of artistry, philanthropy, and societal impact into a cohesive masterpiece.

Future Aspirations: Art, Advocacy, and Beyond

As we peek into the artist's sketchbook of aspirations, Richard Hutchins' future unfolds with a vision that extends far beyond the canvas. This chapter delves into his plans for the art world, advocacy, and personal growth. The Hollywood Hills, once a distant dream, become the launching pad for endeavors yet to be unveiled.

Richard's journey is not static; it's an ever-evolving narrative. The future holds promises of speaking engagements in Chicago, participation in Art Basel in Miami alongside renowned art collectors, and collaborations that position his art next to the works of Warhol and Basquiat. The artist's dreams, once confined to Skid Row sidewalks, now traverse the echelons of the art world.

Painting a Legacy: Leaving a Lasting Impact

As we approach the concluding chapters of this book, Richard's future aspirations become integral to the legacy he envisions. Beyond the strokes of a paintbrush, his ambitions are rooted in creating a lasting impact—both within the art community and the broader landscape of societal change.

This chapter isn't just a preview of events and aspirations; it's an exploration of the artist's evolving identity and the threads that weave his story into the fabric of the future. As we step into "The Pink Party" and gaze upon the horizon of what lies beyond, the canvas of Richard Hutchins' life continues to expand, inviting us to witness the chapters yet to be written and the masterpieces yet to be painted.

Conclusion

In the final strokes of this narrative brush, we find ourselves standing at the crossroads of Richard Hutchins' extraordinary journey—from the unforgiving sidewalks of Skid Row to the illustrious heights of Hollywood Hills. This chapter serves as the crescendo, the epilogue to a story that transcends the confines of a single life and becomes a collective testament to the power of resilience and hope.

Summarizing a Tale of Transformation: From Homelessness to Hollywood

Richard's journey is not merely a chronicle of personal triumph; it's an odyssey that encapsulates the indomitable spirit of human resilience.

From the humble beginnings of Skid Row, his story unfolds like the turning pages of a captivating novel, each chapter marked by challenges, triumphs, and unexpected encounters that transformed a life lived on the fringes into one embraced by the spotlight.

The canvas of Richard Hutchins' life is painted with hues of struggle, tenacity, and the transformative power of art. The LOVE & DREAMS art show, Oprah's surprise endorsement, and the transition from Skid Row to Hollywood Hills—all become strokes in a masterpiece that reflects not just the artist's evolution but a broader narrative of possibility and redemption.

Emphasizing Enduring Messages: Resilience and Hope

As we draw the curtains on this immersive journey, the enduring messages echo like a melodic refrain—resilience and hope. Richard's story isn't a fairy tale; it's a living testament to the belief that dreams, even when trampled upon by the harshest realities, can endure. The sidewalks of Skid Row may have been the stage, but the dreams painted on those streets became the stepping stones to a future unimaginable.

The concluding chapter invites readers to reflect on more than just the life of an artist; it's an exploration of the universal themes that bind humanity—the ability to rise from the depths of despair, find solace in the creative process, and weave dreams into the fabric of reality.

It's a celebration of the indomitable human spirit—a spirit that resonates not just within the confines of Skid Row but across the world.

In bidding farewell to the narrative of Richard Hutchins' life, the invitation is extended to carry forward the enduring messages of resilience and hope. The book closes, not as a conclusion to a story, but as an opening to the countless stories waiting to be discovered, painted, and celebrated. The canvas of inspiration continues to expand, urging us all to pick up our brushes and add our strokes to the ever-evolving masterpiece of the human experience.

Epilogue

As we turn the final page of this narrative, the Epilogue serves as a bridge between the chapters that unfolded and the ongoing journey of Richard Hutchins. This concluding chapter provides updates on his ongoing artistic endeavors and offers closing thoughts on the enduring impact of a story that has transcended the confines of pages and touched the hearts of readers around the world.

Continued Artistic Journey: Brushes, Canvases, and Beyond

The Epilogue takes us into the present moment, where Richard Hutchins continues to wield his brushes, breathe life into canvases, and shape the contours of his artistic identity.

Updates on his current projects, exhibitions, and collaborations offer a glimpse into the vibrant tapestry that continues to unfold.

From the halls of prestigious art galleries to the intimate spaces of his studio, Richard's art continues to evolve. The story that began with envelopes and makeshift materials has now expanded to include a diverse array of mediums, each stroke echoing the resilience and creativity that define his journey.

Closing Thoughts: A Story's End and Beginning

As we bid adieu to the formal narrative, closing thoughts echo the enduring impact of Richard Hutchins' story. The Epilogue becomes a reflection on the transformative power of storytelling—the ability of one individual's journey to inspire, uplift, and instill a profound belief in the human spirit.

Richard's story doesn't conclude with the final chapter; it extends into the hearts and minds of those who have walked alongside him through the pages. The enduring impact lies not just in the strokes of his art but in the universal themes of hope, resilience, and the boundless possibilities that emerge from the fusion of dreams and determination.

The Canvas Continues to Expand: A Call to Action

The Epilogue closes with a call to action—an invitation for readers to engage with the ongoing chapters of Richard Hutchins' life. Beyond the confines of a book, the canvas of inspiration continues to expand, inviting each individual to contribute their own strokes to the collective masterpiece of human experience.

In this closing chapter, the narrative transforms into a living testament—one that encourages readers to pick up their metaphorical brushes and become active participants in the ongoing story. The Epilogue is not just an end; it's a beginning—an opening to a world where stories, art, and the indomitable human spirit converge to create a legacy that transcends the limitations of time and space.

And so, as we close this chapter and open the door to what lies beyond, the Epilogue becomes a celebration of continuity, creativity, and the enduring impact of a story that will resonate long after the final words have been read.